THE ROARING 20'S VOL.1

The Roaring 20's Vol.1

Debby Curreen

Contents

1 Friendship — 1
2 The Lovely Goodbyes — 19
3 War & the World — 35
4 Life — 51
5 CODA — 61

About the Author — 65

Copyright @ 2025 Grumpy Dog Publishing
Far North, New Zealand
All rights reserved. No part of this book may be reproduced in any manner whatsoever without written permission except in the case of
brief quotations embodied in critical articles and reviews.
First printing, 2025.

1
Friendship

There are no ghosts here

I drift through the winding Jasmine,
like we used to in the "old days",
when I enjoyed having moonlight strolls by a river with you.
Morning brought crepes and lemon sauce,
car rides in a clapped-out Austin,
hitchhiking at night in the winter,
living in a funny little bach,
and then a half-finished house...
these fragments in my mind that have now become ghosts to me,
when the days were made of peppermint chip ice cream
and all of it spent with you.

I make my way back to all the "spots",
up roads, down streets, walking narrow lanes, an empty seashore.
I asked a woman about you and visited a man who knew you,
then I found the orchard beside the pond where we'd lived
but everything had changed.
The pictures in my mind bubbled to the top of a lake
I once called forgetfulness,
then I swam in the sea of forgiveness for myself.

"There are no ghosts here," I said to a stranger,
who was walking by with a spaniel dog.
"Good day for it," he nodded to me.
"I think I'll go home now,"
 I told the dashing clouds above my head.
I waited for the ghosts to whisper, "Stay."
I watched the sunset at Ruby Bay.
I went back to my rented cabin,
and I sent my love a text...

"There are no ghosts here...they're all gone."
He sent this message back to me...
"I miss you."
I waited for the sun to rise over Ruby Bay Store.
I missed him too, and then I said good-bye to the ghosts,
and getting on a place,
I whispered, "I'm coming back" to everything and,
of course, to you.

The bad blood of good Friends

I'm on another night out, in the local cafe,
with my bestie, sipping wine, nibbling nibbles, missing a mate,
lamenting her absence, scorning her loss,
wondering what went wrong,
with her.

But *She* did post something that was private, about us, set to public

"When it comes to friends, it's not all wine and roses,
carrot cakes and drunken choruses,
on a floating boat in the harbour," my Bestie said.
"Sometimes pots get thrown, flowers die,
and the wine gives you a bloody headache."
"The boat makes you seasick?
and there are sharks in the harbour," I offer,
as I am pouring her more sparkling wine.
Rose, the pink stuff,
meant for holidays and chatty talk with "the girls".
Not for funerals, and certainly not for a friend
who posted something private, set to public
"Babes can be bitches," a stranger from another table chimed in.
We looked askance at this someone new.
She drank red. Serious about life then,
or worked too hard, trying to relax on a Tuesday night.
I judged her.
But we smiled and nodded our heads.
"I'm Theresa," she offered her hand to me.
"Like the Saint," my friend gave a gentle retort,
an almost welcome giggle.
There's no such thing as Saints, these days, I murmur to no one.

"Join us," my Bestie says to Theresa and her friend.
And they do.
Blood is thicker than water,
and Friendship is stronger than earth.
We might like these strangers, newcomers,
the saints who drink red on a Tuesday night.
And we enjoy the rest of the evening,
swapping facebook and Instagram details,
it's too soon for numbers...
they're not Friend friends, yet.
I'm suspicious,
my Bestie is gullible and kind.
I can't wait to get home.
There has been enough earth and water and wine for one night,
and the moon is still on the rise.
It's a pink blood moon...more blood in the skies,
to match the wine of saints and fallen comrades.

My Inaugural Little Kitchen Soliloquy

I remember the Post Office in Mangonui
across from the store, beside the shore
where we collected our mail,
cashed a cheque, bought a stamp
stood outside in the morning sun
enjoying a friendly chat,
about this and that.
The telephone exchange nestled out the back,
the place that linked the town as one,
by party line,
one conversation at a time.
Long-short-long, funny ring tones back then.

The Post Office was all business inside,
socialising outside
before we wound our ways home,
by foot, bike or a car driven slowly,
 along that windy, pretty harbour road.
Flame trees hung splendidly in red,
throwing shade on our footsteps ,
protecting our head,
as glorious flowers beckoned birds in for lunch,
allowing nests to be built in their arms.

Now I walk in your door, Post Office,
like it's 1904
many precious years later,
incarnations of cafes and bakers,
bars and meal makers,
we have our own Little Kitchen,

already and waiting to serve us our treats,
coffees, salads, pies just for starters,
where we sit , inside or outside on welcoming seats.
Piping hot coffee,
served with the utmost of care,
 alongside the chats with people, staff, and friends,
all of them loved, all of them dear.
Beneath umbrellas or without,
shooting seagulls with water pistols
seeing locals and calling out,
It's such a delight…
the ambient daily basking, in sparkling sunlight.

Come back inside for the art on the walls,
all local, such talent,
in our melting pot village,
with honey, oils, condiments tucked around the café,
this Cafe has it all.
All for sale and ready to go
Even an author gets a spot,
a special shot in the show.

Nestled away from time, a better pace,
to look at life,
chance talks with strangers,
discovering common ground
as we swap our numbers,
promising, "see you around",
while we continue new chats, outside in the sun,
 and always with reluctance we must go home.

To leave all that enfolds and sustains us...
with a view of the sea,
in the best Little Kitchen,
with Tissa & Cherie xxx

As sure as the iris smiles (for Sylvia)

As sure as the Iris smiles in my garden,
so is my promise to send you, her face.
As she beckons the sun to come down upon the Earth,
to pull out the colours,
that's when I will call, "Whaea, the winter has gone,
come see the spring."

The moment I see the gold unfurl amongst the green
with emboldened stems painting serenity for me, and for you
I will fast-post pics of her happiness to your home.
Faith hope love,
the greatest of these, love,
while iris faces glow in the storms of life.

Here is hope, Whaea,
for a day without clouds
and a Heaven come to earth in the faces
of our garden flowers.

Mumma Bear and Redneck do a Roadie

I was going to Nelson, and Golden Bay too,
I was away for a week there
So, I sent a message to you.
"Hey Redneck, I'm doing a roadie
I want you to come.
Don't worry about money,
I have plenty and some.
(Well, not that much,
So, when we sometimes do takeaways
perhaps we could go Dutch?!)
I booked you a ticket,
for a ride on the plane,
I'll meet you at the airport,
you can't say no, you'd be insane.

I've hired a comfy car,
that will be taking us far,
we'll go to Blenheim and Picton,'
then down to Kaikoura!
I'll show you the mountains,
the rivers and sea,
hopefully whales, and the wildlife that runs free.
Then over to Takaka and the beautiful Golden Bay,
I'll show you all the places
where your mum used to stay.
All the homes and the houses,
a commune or two,
and even some campsites,
where I slept beneath the moon.

Then's it back to our cabin,
in the bush, up a hill,
nestled away, peacefully private and still.
We'll go to some wine bars and pubs,
where hours were wantonly spent,
and even to Motueka Riverside,
where I slept most nights in a tent.
Yes, I will be taking you down,
Mumma's memory lane,
reminiscing and laughing while I roll away the years,
which should entertain you or bore you,
who really cares.
But at the end of our roadie,
while we wait for our plane,
you'll be glad that you joined me
we won't be back here again.
But on the trip home,
while we float up in the air,
we can plan for another roadie,
that we'll hopefully be doing next year

Waiting for a widower

I need to stay off "the net"-
it gets dark out there, and not, "the darknet",
the everyday posts that pop up and up and up,
and sometimes bring you down,
like "IT" the scary clown.
Because there was this post I saw today,
it did quite take my breath away.

There was this lady in a wedding dress,
and in her post, this is what she said,
"I'm waiting for a bridegroom,
 as soon as his wife drops dead.
or the casualty of a recent divorce,
some lucky chap to fill my bed."
Yes, I know my fellow reader,
my mouth fell to the floor,
I wish that was the end of it, but sorry,
there was more.
The post it was on facebook,
it was public for all the world to see,
the lady had tagged a hoard of people,
and one of them was me.
I don't know why she tagged me,
I have no husband, I'm alone,
but maybe she thought if she threw it out there,
her post would lure some poor guy home.

I don't mean to be bitchy,
that's not my intention here,
but as I flicked through her many photos,

there was one of her in her underwear.

I had to show my best friend,
I said, "will you look at that?"
She said, "oh, I know that lady,
she's a crazy, scary cat."
"That's not a surprise," I said to her,
"she shouldn't be out on the streets.
I'm going to report her to the admins,
so, they can review that post and delete."

I'm going to stay off the internet,
it's crazy dark out there,
I'm staying in my garden
it's much much safer there.
I told my friend I'd write about it,
that unbelievable post,
that made her snort her coffee out,
upon her freshly buttered toast.
So, this, my gob-smacked reader,
are my thoughts on the man- hunters everywhere,
it's also an urgent warning that all single men should beware.
I pray to God he keeps new widowers safe,
'cause there are some seriously scary cats out there!

I'm going to Poetry Jail

 I'm off to join the convicts,
because I know I'm going to jail.
I know I promised myself and the world,
I wouldn't write poems about any friend,
but I have,
I just can't help myself,
so, poetry jail will be my end.

I hope to make new friends in there,
someone new to write about.
I hope my words will make them sing and laugh,
and dance and jump about.
I hope I don't upset anyone,
I don't want to get thrown out.
Because where do you go after jail,
when you can no longer stay,
where do the fallen poets go,
when their words cause outrage and dismay?
Is there a dark and dreary dungeon,
where ostracised wordsmiths dwell?
A place to sit and mutter,
a room that smells like hell?

Even though my subjects were anonymous,
you could still guess their names,
I always knew my verses were dicey,
but I still played that slippery game.
My editor tried to warn me,
but her words sailed straight past my ear,
"people can get upset,

so, stop making fun of them with your words,
I'm warning you for the final time,
to please, please do beware."

Of course, I bloody ignored her words,
I paid her warning little heed,
casting silly words around,
until they all caught up with me,
and now I'm going to bleed.
For finally I've written something,
and the person did not find it funny,
that I'd dramatized their misfortune
and even made some money.
"Well, that's what paparazzi do,"
I said in my defence,
"You hypocrites who laugh at other people,
from the safe side of your fence."

I'm being charged with sarcasm,
and mirth, and a touch of slander.
As well as trying to bribe the judge,
who refused my generous backhander.
So, off I go to Poetry Prison.
I'm being locked up for a year,
they're denying me internet, pens and paper,
for my entire time in there.
They're going to be bloody sorry,
when I finally get out,
because I'll hide behind a non-de plume
and use the internet to troll, and curse and laugh at,
all those stuffy fudgers that I missed out.

The tree at Mangonui

 Pohutukawa.
Tree of life.
Beautiful and grand,
idling in the light of approaching dusk,
standing sentient, watchful,
a guard beside the ocean's shore
You hold the pulse of the moon and sea in your arms,
the carefree waves that carry salty promises to me.
I stand on shaky rocks.
Oh, wide and curling waters,
I'm at your mercy.
I pray under a silent sky of blue.
waiting for answers
in the shadows,
tangled in the dappled branches,
as I clutch the rustling leaves of the Pohutukawa.
Tree of Life.

2

The Lovely Goodbyes

The Tangi Rain is over

the tangi rain has stopped,
finally
the earth is sodden and heavy
the pain in our hearts too.
  while our minds swell with memory
our spirits limp through the days as
our rangitahi now rest in the arms of our tupuna.
  the tangi rain is over.

the absent face of the sun
breaks apart dark clouds of grief
that have hung for three days
over our whenua.
  shade
we never asked for
unbidden, strangling
pain
wailing goodbyes
dearly departed lifted away into the skies.
  It feels like the tangi rain goes on forever.

the sun shines
drying the last drops
from a silent cross that's
keeping watch, while guiding
  a young soul on the path to eternity.
Te Rerenga Wairua sends thunder
waves beat the rocks with farewells.
  standing on the headland
tossing

goodbyes with roses
arohanui mai
we love you... (come back)

Matariki has begun
our waka is moving across the heaven
Pohutakawa come
and we will meet again in the heavens.
the tangi
the rain
it is now over.

***First prize in the Te Ahu Museum,
Matariki Poetry Competition – 2024**

My Ode to Sinead O'Connor

I will go down to the beach today,
down to the sea on those craggy rocks
to stare the waves down,
dip my toes in ice cold pacific blue water,
to dream for a while and remember you.
I will walk alone across the chilly rocks,
and stare at a silent ocean that shivers and roils,
at the time and tide that is waiting for me.
I will find the darkest rock to perch on
 and hold your life in my arms,
as memories of you gather around me,
singing to me in time with the gentle waves lapping at my feet,
while the pining seagulls drift
on the arctic winds of winter overhead,
I imagine the winds blowing down from Ireland today,
I don't know if that's even true.
But this is an ode, and we're Irish,
so, we can say whatever we want to.

I will stand by the sea today and watch...
the melding colours of aqua depths, swirl,
unfettered and free, as I write something new in my head,
to take home to the table where I will sit,
and think about the books and songs I have yet to write,
the stories and poems I will send out into a world
that might not want me,
I'll play the music that you made and shared,
that you sang into our hearts,
even here, down under, in wee Aotearoa.

I want to say that it doesn't matter what the world says about me,
or what those bastards said about you,
and every other woman with a truth and a voice,
and God help us, when we were given a microphone.
I will use all those rejection letters,
to light my fire on winter nights,
as my dog snores on the couch,
and the last glass and a half of cabernet something or other,
stares at me from a glowering bottle,
before I tip its last drop into my smeary tumbler of misspent joy;
the one that started off as fun,
but later will become the headache of elusive fame,
in the morning after,
when I stare at all those clever lines from the night before.

Yet sleep still comes to me,
and like stars in the night sky,
I twinkle myself into a big bed of dreaminess,
 my solitary, comfortable nest full of my own compassion,
and the dreamy wanderings,
that I share with imaginary, wordy bedfellows,
who are buried beneath my sweaty sheets, next to the dog.
I tuck myself in and tell myself,
I will go back to the sea tomorrow and gather more
stories and songs to bring home;
to bind up into my beautiful life that is not for sale,
or to become pickings for a carnal, snarling, unbelieving world.
I will carry my legacy home from the beach,
and leave it on the shelf with my memories,
the framed photos of everyone I ever lost,
and the souls I managed to keep.

Then later when I am gone, just like you, Sinead,
and every other woman that ever had a truth and a voice,
and if we were lucky, a microphone.
all the world will read or listen to the words we left behind
and they will all say, "she was pretty good, aye?
No wonder she was famous."

**RIP Sinead - now you can, "sleep with a clear conscience,
you can sleep in peace"*

Back row rebel

It's your birthday today,
you would have been 70 and it feels ridiculous now.
to think about all the mad things that we did when we were young,
but hey, I've penned a few words for you,
sprinklings of love, like toppings on a donut,
spreadings of jam on pikelets,
a cool ginger ale at the end of a spring night.
Because my heart leaked on the pages for you,
when you went away,
violently snatched from us,
one terrible Friday in March 2019,
just before my birthday (which was two Saturdays later).
That month feels ruined now
but still,
I have the chaos of colour that was you,
the joyful noise that filled a room from your lips,
memories locked down inside my heart.

I run out of words trying to capture you.
I wrote a book of poems
and dedicated it to you and gave you a whole chapter,
at the back.
cause while you were a front row diva,
you rarked it up in the back -
a Back Row Rebel.
Lines for Lynn, Poems for Pikelet,
a Shout for the Shaheed that you were.
Now a void in the world,
an unmendable tear in my heart.

Our life was lived through letters and road-trips
in cars so illegal it would make a possum's hair curl,
while your mother, "tsk tsk tsk'd"
and we just laughed and laughed,
and rolled around on your big purple bed together.
Gone baby gone...so you are,
and it will take the rest of my life to process all we had,
all I lost
and everything I didn't say.

Still, wise and peaceful sage that I am
here's another poem about you,
for you,
to poke fun and have a larf,
have a cry,
while I write another book
with just maybe...
a chapter in the middle,
for the Back Row Rebel that I loved.

***R.I.P Pikelet** *aka Linda Armstrong*

The night the tui came for you

The sun is bright,
and a soft wind blows calmly through your window,
I say, "Listen to that singing outside, what can it be?"
"It's the tuis,' you say,
"they're waiting for me."
"But not today," I said, and you laughed with me,
"not today, I'm not ready, they will have to wait."
I agreed, no one was ready yet, and you stayed for a while longer.

They returned the next day, and the next,
those tuis sang together,
and we came to enjoy their boisterous chorus.
"They're still here," I told you.
"Yes," you said, "but it's sunny,
 so they can just stay in the trees and cry,"
We laughed together, as we watched the tuis in the kowhai,
harmonising together,
in the branches that touched the sky.

I stand over you, some days later,
the sky was grey, and the clouds hung lower than broken hearts,
you were gone,
leaving us quietly in the early morn.
I looked in the kowhai, but the tuis were also gone.
You had beaten them at their own waiting game-
you'd dodged their songs,
in the dawning light, you had gone.
I had to have a little laugh,
and I sang a quiet song.
You have gone but you'll never be forgotten,

you have left memories, colourful and strong.
And together we outwitted the tuis,
they were too late, the night they came for you,
angels beat them to it,
while I slept deeply next to you.

Now you'll listen to the birdsong in heaven,
yes, you will.
But I am going to miss you,
while that kowhai tree stands still.
and at night when I am all alone,
I cry softly and sing adieu,
then chuckle to myself about how you fled,
the night the tuis came for you.

For Beryl S xx

How can I say good-bye to you

As I stand in the place of our meeting,
a paddock of winnowing golden grasses,
summer winds stroke my arms,
while tall, silent mountains smile down on me,
their whispering voices speak to my heart.
I feel everything,
as I kneel beside a riverbed of yesterdays.
I wait at night for the ghosts to embrace me, wondering.
How can I say good-bye to you?
Every you and every day,
all the moments held in crystal nights,
a love that never left,
but waited here for me until today.

In the town where we met,
on the streets that melt under the summer sunshine of January,
on a new year's day.
I visit hallowed homes, up winding driveways,
my feet tussle with the dust and memories of forty years.
All that is mine, I have carried with me until now…
the pulsing air that I can barely breathe,
as all this magnificence welcomes me back to,
Home.
Time may never wait again for this day.

That night there is a full moon ,
while I lie in a strange bed and stare out a familiar window
listening to the river singing the songs that I have carried,
in my heart all these years,
and my spirit sings through the night while I sleep.
I wake to your laughter, but I am dreaming,

only the birds talk to me while the sun rises.
How can I say good-bye to you and leave behind,
all that is dear and the biggest life I ever had,
a time that changed me forever until now.

I travel over a mountain of marbled memories,
with a friend that I have barely seen for forty years,
someone that was a part of you'
and has now become a piece of me.
The ocean waves have washed my soul,
with a light I've yearned for,
bringing me healing.
I murmur the words that were trapped in my heart,
now free to be released into this wide bay of remembrance.
Even low tide looks good down here,
the rain is friendly, and
I think I can say good-bye.

I have spent a week looking for you,
behind every tree,
beneath sunrises and sunsets and pieces of river slate,
in the blooming dahlias and tangled blackberry vines.
The river keeps flowing through life,
stirring leaves and churning bubbles of a water
almost too pure to drink.
But still, I wonder where you really are.
Memories fall by the wayside of long-ago happiness.
I won't leave you here,
with the ocean, river, mountain, sea and snow,
nights of wine and honeysuckle.
All of it comes with me,
to carry forever,
and I will never say good-bye to you.

The light in my heart that was you

There is a light in my heart,
that searches for you,
in a dark place of loss
where the earth no longer holds colour,
only shadows of a thousand yesterdays
while faint laughter carries across eternity
teasing my memories.

The light in my heart listens,
for that song rolling out on the radio,
notes and lyrics pulling me back to those days of
dancing, leaping, shouting,
our spontaneity making the kitchen a dance floor of
sweat, laughter, alcohol, heartbeats, more.

The light in my heart holds,
my last email to you,
the final poem I wrote,
a shirt that you made for me,
black and gold, too small now,
and a handful of photos of you, always smiling,
always dressed up, colourful and gay,
happy beside me.

The light in my heart remembers,
all the times you stayed with me,
the houses that we lived in,
parties, dinners, all night raves and movies,
every single place we ever went,
the footpaths where we ambled arm in arm,
children running ahead,

a cat, a dog,
added company for our lives.

That light in my heart now cries,
for all the days we shared,
the nights we would hang out together.
I can still feel the tendrils of longing
for the months we spent apart,
shivering despair, for the years where I lost you.
and the wonder of finding you,
all over again,
after so many, many years.

Then one ordinary Friday morning in autumn
across 19 minutes
the news tore my soul
as I teetered on a furious knife edge of disbelief,
My tears raining like bullets,
 your flame was extinguished,
my joy indefinitely muted and quashed.

Five years later,
it's once again another ordinary Friday morning in autumn.
But I hold my breath and cry for those 19 minutes
that destroyed the love,
and took away,
the light in my heart that was you.

*for Linda xx

3

War & the World

War Words

I try to forget war.
I try to remember to forget it but my memories,
and the news, my mother telling (again)about the mustard gas.
My sons play Call of Duty on the PlayStation,
shooting animated humans with high powered rifles.
"It's much worse that that in real life," I tell them.
"Imagine shooting some in the head,
their brains ricocheting off that building."
The "shh" me and push the door in my face.
"It's murder," I shout through the gap in the door frame.
"Bloody murder!"
So much for not remembering war.

I kick a pot plant over,
the flowering succulent my mother-in-law couriered to me,
on my birthday.
She has sent me war in a red van.
Red for a badge of courage,
swaying poppies in a faraway field,
blood on the hospital floors in Gaza,
where the bombs are delivered daily
in black planes by their neighbours,
fall in the hallways of the sick and infirm.
How can I un-memorise war?

So I go outside and stare at an empty sky.
I send up a bomb of prayers to a God,
who may be more confused than me,
and wonders daily, "Where did all this war come from?
How can I stop the murder?"
"I don't know, God," I reply.

My words feel bluer than the sky above
and bleaker than the draining hope in my memories.
What will ever stop the war and images in my head?

"When our soldiers go out on the battlefield,
the have to win," my dad tells me.
"Or they don't come home."

My study is my battlefield.
I am a keyboard warrior,
and I must win this war of words,
weave some lines of hope for the world.
But on win the war today.
I share these frugal lines,
and afterwards...I go home.

In the shadow of a cursed coalition

I've been watching the news again on the terror-vision,
the window of doom
into my sitting room,
and I wonder if anywhere is sacred anymore.

Do the sea lions know they are no longer protected?
That some fullah too fat to fish anymore
is taking away their lives,
while children begin to starve on the playgrounds.

Who really cares? Shrugs a heartless coalition,
 as a couple of politicians turn their coats over on potholes
they're never going to fix.
 'Cos it's time for their five-course lunch, paid for by taxpayers.
"Watch out kiwi and kakapo," cries a bellbird,
 swinging from a brittle kowhai branch,
 as pine trees tagged for China, fall around her home.
"You'll be next!"

Raise your one-use cups of latte to a crumbling sky that doesn't know whether it's raining or crying for the death of the seas it'sposed to water.
 "Water, water everywhere," weeps a lifeless desert, forgetting the rest of the words to a song that extinct generations once sung.
 Forests of amazon proportions once stood here, amidst villages of hearty families who never had to beg or feel the cold touch of colonialist's disease.
 The capitalists take away, then give from thrones of grandiose charity, patting each other's smooth backs while their cavity-free teeth glisten into the cameras while the scales of justice are twirled and twisted by an arctic wind in the middle of summer.

Karma is a lazy bastard sitting on a polished pew in a religious building that he drove his tesla to this morning.

But Mercy watches, and her hand rocks the cradle of a world that heaves anxiously back and forth, and the faithful saints sing, "She's got the whole world, in her hands…she's got the whole wide world… in her hands…"

And we can sing with her, lifting our voices to a heaven that does exist and be glad for the days that she has made, and leave the shadows that a cursed coalition tried to throw on our lives and over our prayers.

Because dogs don't bite the hand that feeds them, but they sure do tear off the hands of the thieves that come at night, and liars' pants do catch on fire and the love of money is the root of all evil …

So ye cursed ones of the coalition, beware…the sword you use to cut today will be the sword that impales you tomorrow.

R.I.P if you can.

My first Anzac Parade

When I was a girl, 5 or 6,
we went to our first Anzac Parade,
just we three -my brother, my mother and me.
Because "your Grandad fought in the war,"
which made me think he went to this Anzac war
But no, not that one, another one. Another war?
How many wars? My little mind boggled.
And he was gassed by mustard gas,
which sounds like something I will never like the taste of.
Now he's in hospital, in an oxygen tent,
where he can no longer hold my hand - because of war.

It was hot, that day of my first parade.
The soldiers wore uniforms the colour of dying grass,
heavy medals clinked beneath the strong sunshine,
as my sweaty hand sought out my mother's trembling grasp.
I awkwardly shuffled from toe to toe, wandering if Santa Claus
was coming to this parade, hopefully to throw some lollies to me.
Mother saluted the steadfast soldiers as they strode silently past,
I raised my hand in a bent salute, shielding my eyes from the sun.
Was this what Gallipoli was like?
I didn't think that I would ever like war.

We went straight home,
marching past my school. No stops,
no treats from the dairy,
and my little brother started to cry.
I hissed, "shut up!" and my mother growled at me for swearing,
on Anzac Day.
I began to hate war.
I practiced my own march along the footpath to our house,

but lacking coordination,
I skipped and danced to my own drum.
Not very warlike.
"You'd never be a good soldier," my mother murmured to me,
critically true, like mothers sometimes do.
I didn't suit compost green clothes.
"Fine by me," my little self silently answered her.

My dad never went to war, nor my brothers,
my sons have stayed home too,
and I hope my grandsons never go.
"Shoot pheasants and turkeys instead, grow vegetables, make art
and music. Do good unto others, win *those* wars," I tell them.
Yet, honour still, those who went,
those who fell and the many who still came home.
And march we will, once a year, LEST WE FORGET!
While raising a flag;
we salute and plant another cross beneath a granite memorial,
as we stand and celebrate the peace those soldiers won.
The men who marched in heavy green uniforms, on hot days,
doing for others,
so that we can have freedom and
live.
Free.

Ban war

...and all who sail on that stinking, sinking ship
of fools with muskets, swords, swearwords, filthy rum and murder.
Those killers on every continent,
waking at dawn, having a yawn,
grabbing guns, making puns
about how many lives they're going to slay today.
Bloody fools.

They tried to ban the bomb, you know,
decades ago,
women especially, didn't want to lose another son,
 another brother
or see their sister place the cap of widowhood
on her stooped and weeping head.
"BAN THE BOMB" the masses shouted,
flags, posters, banners touted, and the protesters marched
and marched, for miles and days,
wearing out footwear,
their cries and the music slowly gathering,
into a worldwide malaise.

"Give peace a chance," John Lennon sang.
We all sang along, clapping, chanting, hoping, praying.
Come and lay down your weapons,
your nightmares of destruction,
wrought by dirty rotten governments trying to rule the world,
and not save it.

And we're all out of words as we pass a tatty baton,
that's somehow survived centuries of bloodshed and carries
the dust of our ancestor's bones, and hope,
the sacrifices and loyalty of men who tried to save the world,
not kill it......and yet, if you listen closely
 daffodils still call hello from the earth you thought was dead.

I don't watch a lot of news, anymore

I don't watch a lot of news, anymore...
or read a paper with bold headlines,
beating me about the face with gloom, death
ricocheting around the globe,
storming my brain, filling the air that I breathe
which creates a world of pain,
for life,
as we now know it.

It makes me blue, the news...
red with anger,
black with sadness,
as real-life images from the battlefields of families,
struggling in the furnace of affliction,
bombard me,
 until it feels like the end of the world inside my soul.

So, I quit the news, for golden
snatches of peace in my heart...
gathering like autumn leaves on the earth,
sending glittering rays of hope and solace into my mind.
I've blocked that drain,
the misery they call news...
with carefree trips to the ocean,
walking in the hills,
picking handfuls of freesias,
with their heaven-sent fragrance that floods my house.

I have filtered my internet letterbox,
halting the scourge of alerts and highlights.
I play gentle music of the heart,

kaleidoscopic daydreams are the perks
of a headline free life.

I don't watch the watch the news anymore.
I lie down in peace.

An acceleration of madness

The skies outside are burning,
the grass on my lawn has been swallowed by Mud.
Down the road, there are highways of mayhem,
bolts of public opinion jam the flyovers,
thoughts are rear-ended by vehicles of outrage every day,
bottlenecks of conflict and arguments.
There is an acceleration of madness in the world right now,
coming to a town near you.

Screens flicker all day long with ultra-violent beams
of mottled truths and sticky facts,
brainwashing dialogues roll up and down
blurring our vision.
Accelerated madness
sashaying daily in the pockets of our youth,
swinging in the handbags of middle age,
sliding across the dashboard of the uber I now sit in.
Pop goes the weasel of reason.

However,
on the flipside of chaos
where calmness still walks,
we find children, candy cane, popcorn and music.
There are parks with lily ponds and swans who sing
a song of redemption to a future
glowing on the horizon of our souls.
A place called hope, a street called love,
a garden full of fresh salad for survivors of accelerated madness.
Water so crystal clear, it puts out every fire
in an aching mind and singed and painful heart,
quelling every argument that exalts itself against the Truth.

Chaos and calm cross swords,
peace and peril punch it out,
while a volcanic victory erupts on man gone mad.
It's the end of the world, baby,
but not what we wanted or even asked for
in the best of our dreams.
The finished work is done,
a new day begun.
Pray, I meet you on the flipside,
the opposite of madness.

Signs in the sky at the end of the world

These first days of the 21st century are like a mighty,
rushing wind, with fiery tongues
as thunder rolls across the ocean's floors, and moons
turn blood red in the sky, or hang blue
in the heavens on sacred nights
while the sun is darkened at midday, by the shadow
of a dog that never bit no one as we ask for a sign,
and the universe plays hiphop.

An iceberg shatters in the North and drifts slowly
into a trembling eternity, while we all dance like
there is no tomorrow, rolling in beds
of wealth that we never deserved, poached from the lives
of families we never knew.
I wonder about hope, as I sit outside a church waiting for
a sign from clouds that obscure the heavens.

They found a polar bear in a rubbish dump
in Siberia, what a hell! She'd lost her babies,
somewhere in the smog of humanity. How did it come
to this? I cried on David Attenborough's shoulder,
while he turned another page, folding it over on
mankind's crumbling destiny.

I paid the invoice for my "mixed recycle bin" the other day, it felt
like a high price to save a failing planet, but then later I swam
in a sea of goodness over sands that sparkled
beneath waves of happiness,
and told God I could live here forever.

And driving home in my vehicle, that sprayed fumes
of poison on the struggling daisies along the roadside,
I asked myself, is there still hope on this rosy,
gentle autumn day.

I watched some irises push through the dirty
ground beneath a laden guava tree, outside in my scruffy
garden.

I thought there might still be life and joy
in a world eclipsed with greed. That there's still a fat chance of

hope.

4
Life

Shooting the bullsh*t

I have no self-esteem...
is a laughable line, from a terrible time,
inside a dream that soon went dark,
and I found my life and all that was dear,
slide down the plughole,
into a terrifying nightmare.

Like Stephen King had come to stay,
bringing monsters that wanted to play,
inside my head and with my heart,
as they messed with my hopes my desires...
they were running around,
all through the house
trying to turn my whole life into fire.

I pushed them away, I closed the door,
I forbade those creatures from crossing my floor.
When down the chimney flew some bats,
python snakes and tricked out cats.
"We've come to take your esteem away,
we're going to make your confidence pay."
I looked at them, well fancy that,
they'd pissed me off, I'd deal with that.
I got my gun, I shot them down,
their screams were heard all over town.
"She's shooting bullshit," the locals said,
"I hope she got them in the head."

I sat down in my comfy chair,
I looked at the carnage and gave a sigh.
They had wasted their time,

coming around here,
I hadn't had any self-esteem for years.
I gave it up a long way back.
I'd tied it up in an onion sack,
I took it down to the out-going tide,
throwing it in, I waved it good-bye.

No, I've got no self-esteem,
I'm too smart for that,
I sorted out those beggars and demons,
the slithery snakes and those cats.
"Pesky bloody monsters," I chuckled to myself,
"they can't take what I ain't got," I said, laughing some more,
bolting my solid back door,
while I placed my loaded shotgun,
carefully back on the shelf.

I miss summer

I miss Summer,
with all her rays of warm sunshine, falling
down on me, calling to me from
the beach where the waters say, "swim, swim, catch this wave...
and this one and this one",
while sand teases my toes beneath a cloudless sky of happiness.

"Come back Summer," I murmur,
 shivering beneath the heavy blankets
of a winter morning, while the temperature reads 4 but feels like
2 degrees of "stay inside".
It's still cold and dark out there,
the clouds let the heat escape during the night.
I think the sunshine has gone to Bermuda,
kidnapped by the triangle.
How will we ever ransom her back?

Four degrees, feels like three, must be two.
I'm not ready to go out into that day without summer,
my friend, my hot companion.
The season that makes life fun.
"Please come back," I say,
wiping the condensation from my eyes.
"Drive the mud away, bring back the flowers."
I miss you Summer, I say to myself, one last time,
shaking my heart up,
before I go in search of Spring.

Last glass of karma, anyone?

"Last glass of karma, anyone?" says the waiter,
 at the end of the year.
"I'll have one," I signal to him.
"Will that be with or without a slice of lemon?"
"Depends?"
Is it sour? I wonder to myself, questioning the universe,
and God above,
that laughing bitch called Life,
and the Mistress of Karma.
"Could I have a cherry instead?"
Our waiter nods nods.
"A sweet one please,"
I murmur to the burnt grass roots beneath my vegan sandals.
Just joking.
My sandals aren't vegan,
neither are my intentions.
The burnt grass bothers me though.
It didn't deserve this.
How innocent is the grass and the planet?
Gaza, the Ukraine, the homeless on the Auckland streets, and all the Americans who got duped into voting for an orange man, instead of a black woman.

I might skip the glass of Karma.
"Give me whiskey on the rocks, smooth ones,"
I say, "the rocks and the whiskey."
I anoint my heart with oakiness,
and settle back to wait for what happens next.

I think humanity has surpassed Karma,
and it's time for a fiery reckoning...
in my humble opinion.
Here's three cheers to karma free years!

In the scrappiness of winter

there is beauty in the garden,
glowstick bursts of colour,
as if Heaven herself has painted the earth this morning,
reflections of hope,
inklings of spring.

I look to the skies, and I see a rainbow of happiness
beaming beneath the heavy clouds
with a promise of more sun shinings
for the morrows yet to come.
I praise winter for the rains
while birds sing in barren trees
joyous and alive
grateful that worms still wriggle, and bugs still crawl
so, there is breakfast again this morning.

Yes, the mud still puddles
and the sky tries to smile,
while the clouds begin to part, and I wear gumboots outside
searching for hope and glory again,
amongst the scrappiness of winter in the garden.

grasping at the wind

I grasp at the wind
in Spring equinox days and longer nights,
while humanity counts their achievements over
twenty-one centuries of civilisation...
and the ground warms up
the seas swell higher
and the world has lost its kindness.

I live by an empty church,
where the graveyard holds more life.
I pick fresh flowers by the headstones,
my dog chases a rabbit into wild bushes.

Puffy clouds hold the balance of
sunlight and rain,
hail scatters outside new buildings full of neon.
Yet bombs fall from that same sky
and children cry in the dirt.
But there are blossoms
petals fall at my feet,
yesterday a rainbow arced over a highway full of potholes
while my car kept moving.
I say my prayers,
and wait for answers...
a fat pigeon sings on my fence.

Then the wind blows warmly through my hair...
fulfilling dreams of justice.

5
CODA

A final glass of doom & gloom

It's nearly midnight,
another year over,
more war than before
and job losses in every town.
Doom is going up
gloom is not coming down,
only acid rain and people's hopes.

It's almost midnight,
the new year is minutes away,
as are the expectations of man,
women are cynical realists,
the hands that prayer and rock the cradle of the world.
Tomorrow is not the magic wand we yearn for.

Midnight is here,
I raise my glass to 2025, but I see a chip on the rim,
not the good omen I peered through my champagne for.
I avoid the chip and swallow all my bubbles at once,
trying not to choke on the fallen world I see outside.
I have enough money to catch an uber home.

Last glass of doom and gloom for the stinky year behind us now,
no better than any other, and maybe better than the next.
Women need six hands to save the world,
just like we need a miracle.
"I'll take another drink," I say to the bartender,
"and give me a fresh glass without a chip."
I'll never get an uber home now.
Farewell 2024, you silly bastard.

Debby Curreen has spent most of her adult life the Far North of NZ, in the Mangonui/ Doubtless Bay area.

Debby started self-publishing in 2018 with her definitive poetry collection, 'The Long Cold Nights of June', telling her story of healing after her youngest brother died from suicide in 2006.

She published two more poetry collection, "I must not write poems about my friends" in 2020, and "Thank you for the words" in 2022, plus a short story collection in 2022 called "Break all my falls", which has uniquely New Zealand themes and some of the stories interconnecting.

She completed her first novel in 2024 which is currently in the early submission stages with publishers.

She has had poems included in several Northland anthologies and in Iona Winter's 'Liminal Gathering' almanac in 2023.

Debby regularly holds regular Spoken Word & Poetry workshops, and enjoys encouraging other writers on their writing journeys.

In 2024 she won the Te Ahu Museum, Matariki Poetry competition.

www.ingramcontent.com/pod-product-compliance
Lightning Source LLC
Chambersburg PA
CBHW022022290426
44109CB00015B/1272